Dream Voyages

REVISED & EXPANDED EDITION

Dream Voyages

John-Roger

Mandeville Press

Los Angeles, California

Published by Mandeville Press
P. 0. Box 3935
Los Angeles, California 90051

Printed in the United States of America
by BookCrafters
Chelsea, Michigan

I.S.B.N. 0-914829-31-9

Contents

There is a lot of speculation about what goes on in the dream state, and there are many theories about the significance and interpretation of dreams. As you read this material about dreams, you may find that some of it seems familiar to you or that you already know a lot of it—up to a point. From that point on, however, you may find that there are some things here that are new to you.

As various ideas about dreams and dreaming are presented in this book, you may start experiencing or recognizing these processes. If this information works for you, you are free to use it. If it doesn't work for you, you are free to disregard it and go on to something that does work for you. Consider the probability that what you read here about dreams is possible. Leave yourself open enough to accept the information in this book. Then, after you have checked to see if this information works for you, you can decide whether or not you believe it.

If you want to receive full benefit from your dream experiences, it is important that you keep track of your dreams. Write them down. Keep a notebook and a pencil or pen by your bed. When you wake up, record your dreams or your impressions of what has happened during the night travel. At first, you may remember only fragments; if you continue to record your dreams—even fragments—you may begin to remember more and more. As you record them, bringing them into conscious awareness, the symbolism of your dreams will become clearer to you, and you will become more skilled at interpreting your dreams.

If you do not remember your dreams at first, just write in your journal or notebook each morning, recording any impressions or fragments that come to you. If necessary, make up something. At first, it may be nothing more than "I woke up feeling sort of uneasy and didn't particularly want to face the day." Or it might be something like "I think I remember seeing a house." That's okay. You just start this process wherever you are, and keep going. If you go for a while without remembering your dreams, don't get discouraged. Just keeping a daily journal will allow you to tune in to new insights about yourself and the process that is your night travel experience. Memory of significant dreams can come in time.

If you are one of those who remember their dreams vividly and in great detail, you may want to be selective about what you write and choose to record only those dreams that seem significant for some reason. For example, if you work as a secretary and have a lot of dreams about typing and filing, these may be nothing more than the subconscious mind attempting to resolve pressures from work. You may choose not to record that type of dream at all, or you may choose to make only a brief notation: "More typing and filing." As you work with this book and your dream journal, you'll discover how you can use them for your highest advancement. The key is to use them.

Psychologists and psychiatrists have been watching the process of sleeping and dreaming for many, many years, trying to find out what goes on in the dream state. They have come a long way in their research and have a lot of information about, and awareness of the dream process. There are, however, some areas of Spirit that are an integral part of dreaming that scientists have not yet become aware of.

Freud popularized dream interpretation and brought forward much in the way of dream symbology. He reserved it as the domain of psychiatric and psychological experts and placed it all within rather narrow limitations. Edgar Cayce really opened up the investigation of dreams and put dream interpretation back into the hands of the dreamer. But both men, although they made tremendously significant contributions to the understanding of dreaming, only went so far. I'll go briefly into what they have discovered and then take you on to what happens in some of the deeper stages of sleep.

1

Twilight Sleep
and the Dreams
of the
Subconscious Mind

You might think of the waking, or awake, state as being that state in which you are consciously aware of all your physical surroundings and alert in your actions and reactions in relationship to your physical environment. But the line between the waking state and the sleeping state is not hard and fast. There is no definite, clear-cut division between waking and sleeping.

During the day, you normally function in an awake state. Then, in the evening, you usually experience a period of time when you are less alert, less aware of your surroundings than you are when you're in a fully awake state. Yet you may not be asleep. You've probably seen people sit and yawn as they watch television in the evening. They may be half watching and half dozing. If you ask them to describe what they have been watching, they might not be able to give you a clear idea of the program. If you ask them if they were asleep, they might not know for sure. They've been in a sort of in-between state. I'm sure that many of you've experienced this in many different situations.

You may go to bed and decide to read for a while before going to sleep. At some point, you may realize that you haven't been paying much attention to what you've been reading. So you go back a few paragraphs and read them again. Yet when you get to the end of the page, you realize that you still don't know what you read, and you have to read it again. Are you awake or asleep? You're certainly not very alert physically. As you get to this point, you may just put the book down, turn off the light and go to sleep. Then, as you start to truly fall asleep, you lose conscious awareness of your surroundings, and you start moving through other levels of consciousness that are not as available to you when you are awake.

In those first two or three hours (the time can vary) of the sleep state, when you do not have a conscious awareness of your physical surroundings, you are actually in a twilight zone; I call this twilight sleep. It's a light sleep state. You may be just dropping off to sleep and your muscles may start to twitch or jump. You may hit your spouse, who says, "For

heaven's sake, can't you just relax and go to sleep?"
You might snore during this light stage of sleep. You
might wake up a couple of times and check the clock
to see what time it is. In other words, it's a fairly light
and possibly restless sleep state.

During twilight sleep, there is dreaming. The
dreams you have in this stage will probably closely
correspond with the day's activities, and you'll try to
resolve what has happened during the day. If there
is anything that has been left unresolved in some
way, you will try to complete and finish it in your
dreaming. These are the dreams of the subconscious
mind.

For example, someone may have said something
to you during the day that you didn't like very much.
Your subconscious mind may have reached out and
latched on to the slight. It will emotionalize it, pull it
in, and lock it into the memory pattern. Consciously,
you may not even have been very aware of it, or you
may have consciously dismissed it by thinking
something like, "They don't know what they're
talking about, anyway." Subconsciously, however,
you have held on to that comment, so when you go
to sleep at night, the subconscious will try to reconcile
it. You might dream that you hit that person in the
nose, or that you fight with them. You might go
through all sorts of turmoil to complete the action.

If you've had a difficult day at work and have been under a lot of pressure, you might dream of being at work and completing more work assignments or of performing many of the things that you ordinarily do at work—typing, meeting with clients, working on projects, working with tools, etc. Whatever you do during your waking hours, you could find yourself doing more of that in the dream state.

These dreams of the subconscious, because they may be trying to resolve several different areas of your life, can appear to be very confused and scattered. A typical dream might go something like this: You go to work and your boss is there. But your mother is sitting at your desk, and when you go to the other side of the room to use another desk, your wife and kids are there eating breakfast. Then the boss gets really angry, and you become fearful that you'll be fired...and so on. These are dreams of confusion because the activities of the day were unresolved in some way, on some level. If there is anything that was not completed during the day, you'll very often try to work it out in the dream state. One of the reasons that the dream state is so valuable is that it helps you to work out your daily problems and frustrations and to become more comfortable with yourself and your expression.

The dreams of the subconscious mind may also have to do with bodily functions. These are what I call "food dreams." If you have eaten too much food before going to bed, the peristaltic movement of food through the body will cause you to have dreams. If you go to bed very thirsty or very hungry, you may dream about obtaining food or water. This is natural because, subconsciously, you are aware of the needs of the body and will try to fulfill those needs.

Many times, youngsters who have bed-wetting problems will dream that they are in the bathroom, completing the natural process in the correct and acceptable way. Physically they're not, but their dream has been so real to them that they'll say, "But I thought I was in the bathroom." When children feel pressure on the bladder or the stimulation of the pajamas or bedding twisting around the body, they may have dreams that correlate with that pressure on the body.

It's important that youngsters who have a bed-wetting problem go to the bathroom before they go to bed at night. It will also help if they don't have anything to drink after five o'clock or so in the evening and if their bedclothes are arranged so that they will not twist around the body and cause unusual pressures. These precautions will make it easier for children to control themselves.

An adult can also suggest to the child, to their subconscious mind, that they "keep the bed nice and dry and warm" during the night. The suggestion should be phrased in the positive. If you say, "Don't wet the bed," children more than likely will because you have reinforced that action: "Wet the bed" were the last words they heard. Children will usually respond to simple, positive suggestions.

Sexual dreams, for the most part, also occur during this twilight sleep, and most often they are part of a pattern that the subconscious is attempting to resolve. If there is a person whom you find particularly attractive or desirable and the relationship is not a fulfilling one, you may dream of having sex with that person. It might fall into the "wish fulfillment" category. And, as with other bodily-function dreams, it's often the stimulation of the bedding or clothes that can initiate a sex dream.

In dream laboratories, where researchers have watched people sleep and have tested and experimented to determine the process of their dreams, the subjects have not gone below this stage of twilight sleep. Researchers have used several methods of investigation to determine when the people are dreaming and on which level they're dreaming. When a person is dreaming, even though the eyelids are closed, the eyes will appear to be watching what is going on in the dream state and will move back and forth as they follow the action of the dream. Scientists have given this process a name: rapid eye movement, or REM. By using electroencephalographs and other equipment that record brain waves, they've been able to separate and identify about five levels of dreaming within twilight sleep. As they develop more sophisticated equipment that is able to record subtler movements of brain waves, they will discover more levels.

By watching for REM and by identifying changes in brain wave activity, scientists in a laboratory situation can accurately identify when people are dreaming. They'll awaken their subjects and ask what the dream was. The dreamer may say, "I was watching people ride bicycles." Then they'll be told to go back to sleep. The dreamer goes back to sleep and starts dreaming again, is awakened again, asked about the dream, and then told to go back to sleep. All of the dreams that are reported in this stage of dreaming are the twilight sleep dreams of subconscious completion and resolution.

Scientists have found that people who are deprived of sleep and, thus, of dream experience, become disturbed. If the release process inherent in dreaming is disrupted, the subconscious does not have a chance to complete its communication efficiently in the body. People who have not had enough sleep begin to hallucinate and get angry, irritable, and hostile. We all know what happens when someone hasn't had a good night's sleep. The next day they can be like a bear with a sore paw. If people are denied sleep for a long enough period of time, they may become psychotic—not necessarily permanently psychotic, but psychotic for the period of time during which they are sleep-deprived until they are allowed to sleep and dream normally. When they can go to sleep, they will reconcile the imbalances of their lives, and their expression will move back within their bounds of normality.

The subconscious mind stands as a guardian to the consciousness, the conscious self. That is part of its function of completion during the dream state. It is attempting to reconcile for the consciousness what could not be reconciled in the awake state and, thus, to protect the consciousness from undue disturbance and turmoil. Because it serves this function, the subconscious will protect you if it feels any threat at all. If you are being observed during your sleep, it may run protection and not allow your level of sleep to drop too deep. Usually, you will not drop past the twilight sleep if you are being watched; you will stay in a light, restless sleep. This is particularly so if you are being awakened often during your sleep. For these reasons, it is very difficult for researchers to discover the deeper stages of sleep and dreaming that take place within the consciousness.

2

Levels of Dreaming

There are levels of consciousness beyond this physical consciousness. You are probably quite aware of the physical level. Then there is the subconscious level, which we have just been discussing. Beyond those, there is an astral level, a causal (emotional) level, a mental level, and an etheric level. And beyond even those, there is the Soul level. Each level exists both inside of you and outside of you; each is both subjective and objective. Each level may be expressed more completely and with greater perfection outside of you, but each level also expresses itself within your own consciousness.

You have a consciousness on each realm or level. That consciousness is a vehicle for your expression there. On the physical level, your vehicle for expression is the physical body. On each of the other levels, you may not have a body that would be identified as the physical body is identified. It is a body in the sense that it is a vehicle for your expression on each of these realms or levels of consciousness.

The astral consciousness can go out and travel on the astral realm, work through patterns, and perceive and know and be, just as much as you can now, in the physical consciousness. The causal consciousness can travel on the causal realm, the mental on the mental realm, and the etheric on the etheric realm. Each one of them can be on those realms and can exist there in consciousness as fully as you exist here in physical consciousness. You exist on every level of consciousness at all times. You are multidimensional. You are much more than your physical body—much more and much greater.

When you go past the stage of twilight sleep, you go very deeply into these other levels of consciousness. This is the time that you may not know you're dreaming. This is the time when the "spiritual dreams" take place. You may sometimes move quickly past the twilight sleep and into these other levels. When that happens, you might say later, "My head barely hit the pillow, and I don't remember a thing until I woke up in the morning. I don't think I moved all night long. I know something happened during the night, but I don't remember a thing." Because these levels are deep within the consciousness, it is more difficult to bring experiences of them back into conscious awareness.

Astral

As you drop past the twilight sleep, the other levels of consciousness (the other bodies) begin moving out or splitting off from the consciousness of the physical. They travel into the other realms, where there are many kinds of activities and experiences. You usually drop off into the astral body first and travel in the astral realm. Many of the actions in the dreams from this level will be closely associated with the physical realm. The reference points will, for the most part, be from the physical world. You'll see people, animals, and cities much as they exist on the physical. People and places will be more or less physically recognizable.

The lower part of the astral realm is "nightmare alley." Here you may have nightmare experiences, weird dreams of monsters, snakes, and bogeymen, etc. This is where most of your nightmares occur. Because the astral realm includes imagination, you may meet there all the monsters that you have ever imagined. In a sense, you have created there all the things that you've let your imagination dwell on and place negative energy into, and you may meet up with them as you travel that realm. In a way, it's terrific because it gives you the chance to confront them and discover that they are illusions of your own creation and not real at all. When you learn to work with the Light and the Mystical Traveler, you can ask for the presence of the Light and for the Traveler's protection, and you will usually see the monsters dissolve right in front of you. We'll talk about the Light and the Traveler in more detail in Chapter Four, "The Soul's Dreaming".

A typical dream of the astral realm might be finding yourself in a really frightening situation and trying to scream, and no sound comes out. You may try to run away and find that you can't move or that you are running in slow motion. The scenes may shift rapidly. When a monster gets too close, you may suddenly find that you're someplace else. There may be a pervading sense of stickiness or heaviness in these dreams. In the morning, you might say, "I'd like to tell you about this dream, but I don't think I have the vocabulary or the skill or the time."

The experiences on the astral realm may also be highly emotional at times. Your fear patterns, your worry patterns, and your negative patterns are often based in the astral realm. You may have a lot of fear in relation to the astral because you may have been there before and not liked your experience. When your muscles twitch and jump, or when you feel as if you're falling and you jerk as you hit bottom, you are probably moving into the lower part of the astral realm. Sensing, but not necessarily knowing, that you are moving into an area that's not too nice, the consciousness resists going there, and you may find this jerking process going on.

The high part of the astral realm is very beautiful. Many people in metaphysical circles refer to this area as Summerland. It has majestic cities, and the people there are very beautiful. It might be similar to the traditional concept of heaven, with pearly gates, streets of gold, and that sort of thing. If you visit this part of the astral realm, you'll probably enjoy it very much.

Perhaps more than 99 percent of the people on this planet astral travel at night. You don't have to be asleep to astral travel, but it's often easier to travel if the physical consciousness is not active. One way to travel astrally while you are awake is through daydreaming. When you create imaginary situations and scenes in your mind and move through them and they become almost as real or even more real to you than the physical world, you are usually in the astral consciousness. These scenes that you create or have created in your mind may take place in the astral realm.

It's important to become aware of what a powerful creator you are. There is nothing that you put into motion through your mind and emotions that is not recorded somewhere, and these creations will often come back to you when you least want them. It really pays to be very careful about what you imagine, or "image in" to your consciousness.

Causal

The next level of consciousness that splits off from the physical during dreaming is the causal. The experiences of the causal consciousness may still have some elements of the imagination present, but the primary experience will be emotional. You might wake up just loving the whole world. Or you might wake up hating your next breath. These will be keys for you that you have been traveling on the causal realm. Often, you won't remember seeing specific people or places, but you'll have a strong, strong feeling. You might say, "I had this terrible dream. I can't remember what it was about, but I was terrified." Or "I can't remember where I was or what I was doing, but I was in the most beautiful place. It was so nice and peaceful." These are probably from the causal realm of consciousness.

Mental

As you drop more deeply into the sleep state, the mental consciousness may split off and travel into the mental realm. The dreams or experiences you have on this level may seem unusual because you will wake up knowing that you were taught something during the night. You'll know you were in a class. Most often, if you've been on the mental plane, you may not see people or remember particular places. Your memory will probably be more related to ideas, knowledge, and thoughts; it will be a mental process. You may remember hearing part of a lecture or someone reading out of a book, but you may not be able to remember anything of the lesson. You might try paying closer attention. The more information you can bring back from the sleep state, the more valuable these experiences can be to you.

Etheric

The next level is the etheric consciousness, which is very hard to describe. This is neither mental nor Soul, but is in between the two. I don't have words that will accurately describe the etheric experience. On this level, there is clarification of who you are, within your own self. In this realm, there is a testing process to see if you are ready to move into the Soul realm. If you have been traveling on the etheric realm, you may wake up with the sense, "I've got it! I've really got it!" You won't be able to say what, but you'll know it. And that day, you may find yourself flooded with a knowing, a sense of fulfillment, and an overwhelming sense of oneness.

3

Precognitive Dreaming

There is another level of consciousness called the basic self which resides a little deeper than the subconscious mind. The basic self can separate from the physical consciousness and project into the future. It can transcend barriers of time and space and move ahead to take a look at next week, next month, or a year from now. Then, perhaps a year later, you may be going down the street, and you'll turn a corner and say, "I've been here before." The French call this experience *déjà vu*, which means "already seen," having been there before, having done the same thing before. The basic self has seen that scene before.

You may bring back the memory of a precognitive dream as a disturbed or uneasy feeling. You may say, "I feel like something's going to happen. I can feel it in my bones; something's going to happen."

Nothing happens, and your husband (or wife) says, "You're nuts. You had me upset all day long, and nothing happened." The basic self has gone ahead and perceived something that it is either excited or concerned about. It has brought back the memory, but because its job is to protect the consciousness, the conscious memory will be blocked, mixed up with a dream, confused with a past action, or distorted in some other way. But the feeling of uneasiness remains.

Then one day, about six months later (this is arbitrary; it could be three months, a year, or anything else), something happens and you say, "I knew it." There may not be many people who are going to believe you, but you'll know that "feeling," and you'll understand what it was. People who have never experienced déjà vu may have a hard time accepting that this can and does happen, but once they experience it, they'll know what you mean. It becomes a different process of awareness.

When I was young—about fourth, fifth, and sixth grades—I used to have terrible heat, like a fever, come through my body. I know now what it was, but at the time it was just an unknown, unexplainable, tremendous heat that used to shake up my parents. My temperature would shoot very, very high. They'd try to bring it down, and I'd be delirious, raving out of my head. I was really out of the body, but I didn't know it then. I would dream that I saw white things going across the sky. They'd go off in one direction and disappear; then they'd pick up again and appear in another part of the sky. One would break away, and another would appear. I couldn't see what made them, and that bothered me. That was my "fever dream." Many people dream one particular type of dream when they have a fever, and that was mine.

Many years later, I was driving down the road with friends, and we saw the contrail of a jet that was flying overhead. I said, "There's my dream. That's my fever dream. I saw that years and years ago." They looked at the sky and said, "That's right. You described that." As the jet passed, the contrail broke up. We were under a jet pattern, so we pulled off to the side of the road and waited for another jet to fly over. I didn't remember if, in the dream, I had been sitting in a car and looking at the contrails, but I certainly remembered seeing these types of patterns take place.

Was it only a fever dream, or was I seeing ahead? If I had written this down, I probably would have been able to recall it much more exactly. As stupid, silly, and irrelevant as the vision had seemed at the time, it proved to be very relevant. I just hadn't had the wit to see it and know it. We all miss a lot of things that we think aren't worthwhile at the time, only to find out later that they were actually very worthwhile.

There is a second twilight sleep stage that occurs just before you wake up in the morning, and this is the time that most precognitive or prophetic dreams take place. If you can bring back memory of these dreams, you will get a preview of every major thing that will happen to you in your life. You will not have one major thing happen to you that will not first be seen in this morning twilight sleep.

The morning twilight sleep can also be a time of more subconscious dreaming, which will appear very similar to dreams of the evening twilight sleep stage. The memories of both of these stages are often interwoven and confused, and when you wake up, you may have difficulty differentiating between the two stages.

4

The Soul's Dreaming

We haven't talked yet about the realm of the Soul and Soul consciousness. When you reach into the Soul realm, you are reaching into the positive realms of Light, the pure realms of Spirit. The lower realms (physical, astral, causal, mental, and etheric) are negative—not bad, but negative like the pole on a battery that is opposite the positive pole. There are both positive and negative realms of Light, just as there are positive and negative poles on a battery. On this level, one without the other is incomplete, out of balance. When they are put together, they form a whole and become a working, functioning unit of energy and force.

You can travel into the lower realms of Light by your own volition. You can project your consciousness into these realms. How far you can travel in the lower worlds depends on your level of awareness and development. It's a process of evolvement. Many people may never travel higher than the astral realm in the dream state, and they may not even be aware of that. They might not believe you if you told them anything else existed. Potentially, however, everyone has the ability to travel all of the lower realms without guidance.

In the Movement of Spiritual Inner Awareness (MSIA), there is a mystical consciousness that is a focal point of energy and that has the ability to transcend levels and to work with the students and initiates of MSIA on all levels of consciousness, as is best suited to their individual needs. It is through the work of this mystical consciousness that students and initiates can be shown the Soul realm and can, with guidance, traverse all realms of Light in Soul consciousness. Jesus the Christ, who carried the mystical consciousness that works with MSIA, said, "I am the way, the truth, and the life: no man cometh unto the Father, but by me."[1] He meant that it was through his consciousness, the consciousness of the Christ, that each person could be given the keys into the Soul realm, into the realm of pure Spirit. Without the help and the guidance of the Mystical Traveler Consciousness, it is difficult to move into the Soul realm. Because of the way the Soul realm is protected from that which is not pure, it is much easier to go

1. John 14:6 (King James Version)

with one who can show you the way, who can act as your guide.

Each realm of Light has certain delineations, certain rules, certain laws that are particular to that realm. Each realm has a Lord, or overseer, who is responsible to the laws of that realm and for seeing that those within the realm abide by the laws. When you travel in the astral body, you are bound by the laws of that realm, and it is the same for each of the other lower realms. But when you travel in the Soul body, under the protection and direction of the Mystical Traveler Consciousness, you are free and cannot be bound by any of the lower realms. Once you learn how and once you are working with the Mystical Traveler Consciousness, you can step directly from the physical into the Soul consciousness, into the Soul realm. Then you can move back down through all the lower worlds, picking up a vehicle for expression on each realm as you come to it. You will pick up these lower bodies, or sheaths, as needed, while always maintaining the freedom of Soul consciousness.

Those who are students and initiates of the Mystical Traveler have the Soul realm as their goal and may travel in the Soul realm and above during the night travels. Much of their travel on the lower realms of Light is for their learning and growth, and to complete actions they have started in these lower levels so that they are free to travel in what I call the "high country," the Soul realm and above.

When you work within MSIA, under the protection of the Traveler, you are allowed to bypass the lower realms. When you drop into deep sleep, you are immediately pulled into the Soul realm by the Traveler. Then, as you travel down through the lower worlds, you have all your experiences under the Traveler's protection. There is nothing that can hurt you, nothing that can harm you.

Even if you aren't in Soul consciousness, nothing can bother you except those things that you have created. If you create fear, you become fearful. If you create negativity, you become negative. So if you're smart, you'll create love, harmony, balance, good will, and fellowship because these things will then be returned to you. When you travel in the other realms, you meet those things that you have created. Wouldn't it be nice if all your creations were beautiful, positive, and uplifting?

The work of MSIA is about 10 percent on the physical level and about 90 percent on the spirit side, in the realms of Light. In the dream state, which reflects your activity in the other realms of Light, there are continuous seminars going on, continuous schooling, training, and learning. This training is going on all the time—"twenty-five hours a day, eight days a week." If you become aware of these levels, you can consciously receive more and more information from them. They're happening. You have the potential for becoming more and more aware of them and using them as part of your daily living.

When you are working directly with the Mystical Traveler, as a student preparing for initiation or as an initiate into the Sound Current, you will be involved in some experiences in the night travel that will be particular to that relationship.

For example, you may have dreams with the "Traveler" that will be part of your own inner levels, rather than encounters with the Traveler on one of the realms of Light as an outer reality. You may see the form that you identify as the Traveler and experience it as being with you, guiding and directing you. It may be that the part of you that is centered in the Traveler Consciousness is guiding you—and that may be completely valid for you at that moment. A deeper level of you may mock up the form of the Traveler because you will give credence and recognition to that form. If you check those dreams with me, outwardly, I may tell you that I was not part of them, meaning that the dreams took place within your own inner levels. That does not make the dreams invalid. It only means that the dreams were a part of your own inner process.

There are also illusions that can occur in dreams of the "Traveler." If you dream of the Traveler and are open to its guidance, there are a few valuable keys by which you can check the validity of your experience. When you truly see the form of the Traveler in your night travel, that experience will be accompanied by feelings of loving recognition, safety, and protection. If you see the Traveler's form and experience fear or anxiety with it, be aware that it may not be the Traveler. The presence of the Traveler will also be accompanied by an energy that will be joyous and uplifting to you. Another key is that the Traveler will usually appear to you from your right side; occasionally, it will appear from directly in front of you. So if you see or hear the Traveler on your right, that is a pretty good indication that it really is the Traveler. If a form that appears to be that of the Traveler approaches from the left, be careful. If there is any doubt, ask for the Light and for the Traveler and its protection. If the form is false, it will disappear. If you hear what you think is the Traveler's voice and you hear it in your left ear, be very careful about heeding that guidance. Check it out.

Perhaps the most certain way to check the truth and validity of the Traveler's appearance in the night travel is to check the information you receive. The Traveler will never contradict its own teachings. If you are told something in a dream by one who appears to be the Traveler, and it conflicts with the teachings as you know them from the MSIA Soul Awareness Discourses and MSIA tapes and books, you have not been in touch with the Traveler. The inner teachings do not conflict with the outer teachings. They may, however, be an amplification of them.

The Traveler will never counsel you, on any level, to hurt or harm yourself or anyone else. It will never counsel you to cheat or to lie. It will never counsel you to go against the laws of the land, to be destructive, or to be deceitful. The Traveler will never ask you to divulge that which is sacred and secret. If anyone in any form (other than John-Roger, physically, or a member of the MSIA initiation staff, physically) asks you to repeat your initiatory tone on this level or on any other level of the inner or outer realms, you are not dealing with the Traveler or a being of Light. You may say your tone in challenging the spirit that comes to you and tries to beguile you. If it is of God, it will say your tone back to you. If it is not, it will disappear.

It's important to know, too, that there are many levels of illusion and temptation that you may encounter in the dream state. The teachings of this world are not separate from your dreams. What you learn here also applies to those other levels, just as the teachings you learn there apply to this level. The keys you have learned here on the physical level about working with the Light, placing the Light around you for protection, asking for the presence of the Traveler, and chanting your initiatory tone, all work in the dream state as effectively as they do here. So use the tools that you have learned, and apply them to all levels of your existence.

It is also important to realize that there are some very subtle levels of desire and illusion that may be at work within your own consciousness. You may want to do something so badly that your own subconscious or unconscious patterns will attempt to fulfill those desire patterns by mocking up a form that will give you its permission to complete that desire. Then you may feel justified in going ahead and doing whatever it was that you wanted to do. You might say, "Well, I was told in a dream that it was a clear action." It may be illusion born of desire and perpetrated in deceit. Don't be foolish in relationship with yourself. Check your levels and your information, and be honest with yourself. The inner teachings that you are able to remember will always match the outer teachings. The Traveler never supports dishonesty or deceit. The old adage that "dishonesty forfeits divine aid" holds true.

If you receive information you are unsure of which relates to the teachings of the Traveler, be smart and check it out. Write to me or the MSIA staff. If I have been a part of your dream or night travel experience, it's easy for me to verify that for you, and if I have not, it's easy for me to let you know that as well. Don't get caught up in following your illusions, however cleverly they may masquerade as Spirit. A big key is always to keep moving on to the next experience, the next level. If you do that, then even if you get caught up in illusion, you won't stay there. You'll move on through it and keep lifting.

Many people who are on the path of the Sound Current have initiatory experiences in the dream state. Each Sound Current initiation that takes place in the physical will be preceded by that initiation in the higher realms. The initiation on the physical level is the verification of that and the connection of that initiation into this level. If you experience a Sound Current initiation in the night travel, it will be accompanied by a few key points that will identify it as such. One will be the presence of the Traveler, perhaps others who are also initiates, and often members of the MSIA staff who are involved directly in the initiatory process. You will probably experience an intensification of energy that will be noticeable through all the levels, including the physical level. Another key will be a noticeably intensified activity of Light energy in the third eye and/or crown chakra. Often, there will be the memory of the Traveler's hands being placed on your head.

Within each Sound Current initiation, there are many Light initiations. If you are initiated to the causal realm, you will experience and perhaps remember many initiations within that realm. These will be beautiful experiences and may involve the presence of the Traveler. Generally, they will not have the intensity of a Sound Current initiation and will not carry all the keys that will identify them as a Sound Current initiation. If you experience these dreams of initiation and wish to check them out with me physically, through a letter, that's fine. But check your own level of knowing first, and see if the experience is real or a mock-up of your desire.

5

Balancing Past Actions Through Dreaming

Now that you have some awareness and working knowledge of what happens during the dream state and the levels to which you may be traveling, I'd like to go back and fill in a little more information for you.

There is a law that exists throughout all the lower realms of Light, which is the law of cause and effect. That cause and effect is simply action—yours, mine, and that of this physical world and many other realms of existence. It is neither negative nor positive, neither good nor bad; it is action, change, and experience. It is governed by a simple dynamic: As you sow, so shall you reap.

Before coming into this physical existence, you agreed to experience and fulfill certain actions during your lifetime. You don't have to do this with anyone but yourself. You clear actions with yourself, and you come into the physical realm to work them out, balance them, and complete them. Sometimes another person will come in to help you balance your past actions, but each of you could have chosen to balance those actions with other people.

Actions must be cleared and balanced individually, within each person. You can sometimes look into past existences and see where two people who are together now have been together before, but each one still has to clear their actions within themself and bring themself into balance.

There is a master force, or dream master, from the spiritual realms who works with the students of MSIA. One of the reasons the dream state becomes so valuable spiritually is because, through the action of this dream master, you are allowed to balance actions in the dream state instead of on the physical level. How would you like to live through those nightmares in an awake state? Through this special action, many negative actions (like car wrecks, accidents, or other dangerous or threatening situations, etc.) have been bypassed in the physical, and completed on another realm through the dream process.

In the dream state, the dream master will show you the illusions of the dream worlds. He will show you which action is illusion and which is reality. Your learning and your progression can be so much faster when you don't have to find all these things out for yourself.

In the dream state, you may balance actions from your past existences, too. You probably haven't always been the nice person you are now. Most people have done some pretty terrible things to each other and to themselves. It can be awfully shattering to your "spiritual ego" to find out that you were probably considerably less than spiritual in another existence.

You have to pay back your debts; you have to balance your actions. Each time you do balance an action, even if it appears to be through an unhappy or difficult situation, you become more free. As you repay each debt, you move into greater freedom. It is so fantastic to be able to balance these actions on all realms of Light, not just the physical. When you work with the dream master to balance actions, you can clear things up and become free much faster.

As well as having actions to balance on the physical level of consciousness, you may have them on the astral realm, the causal realm, the mental realm, and the etheric realm. So you must work out your debts on every level. You can do this through the dream state.

When you travel in the astral body, you may be balancing actions there, and in the causal body, you may be balancing actions on the causal level. You may be fulfilling the same process on the mental and etheric realms.

There are many levels or frequencies on each realm of Light. For example, there are more than four billion people on this planet right now, and you are strongly aware of some of them, dimly aware of others. If all those people were on the astral realm, you wouldn't necessarily be aware of anyone but yourself on that realm. Here on this level, there is little way to avoid being aware of other beings who are also here on this level. On the astral level, however, if you don't want to see certain people, you will never meet them. Your frequency will be different enough that you will never even be aware of them. The difference in frequencies might be infinitesimal, but enough that you would never meet. This is what Jesus the Christ meant when he said that in his father's house there are many mansions.[2] He didn't refer to "levels of consciousness" because people at that time would not have understood his meaning. They could relate to a mansion, a place to live, a home. The vocabulary is different today; the meaning is the same.

If you are balancing past actions in the other realms, your dreams can become really intense. Dreams of this type, dealing with release and

2. John 14:2 (King James Version)

fulfillment, are often not too pleasant. Many times, the subconscious will block the memory of these balancing dreams and you might be grateful for this, although you may wake up with a lingering sense of depression or heaviness. It's good to keep some water by your bed. If you have bad dreams or wake up with a feeling of heaviness, drink some of the water when you wake up. This will assist you in breaking the connection, in "shorting out" the oppression of the dream. It will clear things quickly and allow you to come back into full awareness and presence here on the physical.

Reestablishing Physical Consciousness

When you come back in the morning from the night travels, you may sometimes hear a pop or feel as if you've been slammed back into the bed. Or you may wake up with a start, your eyes may fly open, and you may be staring at the ceiling, thinking, "What on earth was that?" You might listen to hear if a car backfired or if somebody slammed a door, yet you know that nothing like that happened. You know that the sensation came from inside you.

If you come back into physical consciousness too quickly, your back, shoulder, neck, or head will sometimes ache. You might get out of bed and find that you can just barely hobble around, thinking that maybe it's arthritis or rheumatism or that you're just getting older. It may just be that you slammed back into your body too fast.

Sometimes when you come back into the body, you don't get in completely straight, toe to toe and fingernail to fingernail. When this happens, you get up and walk around in a daze all day long. You may say, "I'm just not very with it today. I'm not all here." That's right—you're not all here. If you feel this way, like you're not back in the body straight, it may help to go back to bed and lie down very straight, with your hands straight down or straight up so that the electromagnetic energy can flow freely, without interruption. Close your eyes and count yourself back into the body. Start with ten, and tell yourself that when you get to one you'll be all together and present in your body. Then start counting down. You might also want to do some physical exercises. Some vigorous sit-ups or push-ups will usually pull you back into the body very quickly.

Another technique for reestablishing physical consciousness is to say the tone of "E" inwardly or out loud a couple of times. Say it as a sustained 'EEEEEEE' sound, starting the voice at a very low pitch and imagining it down around your feet, taking it up as high as you can and imagining it up at the top of the head and then dropping it back down to a low pitch down at your feet. Chanting this tone a couple of times can realign all your energies and get you anchored back down on this physical level.

6

Interpreting Dreams

Dream interpretation can be tricky because you travel on so many levels at the same time. During a single night you may have a dream initiated by the subconscious mind, a precognitive dream, and experiences on the Soul, etheric, mental, causal, and astral levels of consciousness. Then you come into the physical awareness and try to perceive all this with your mind. You might wake up and say, "I had a dream that I was in a motorboat going across the desert, and my aunt was there. She's been dead for twenty years, but I was so happy to see her. Then we saw some Indians in canoes, but they weren't really Indians; they only looked like Indians." Dreams that you remember in this kind of jumbled pattern are usually mixed-up recollections of thought patterns from several different realms. The memories intermingle, and the result seems like confusion.

You might have had a dream about elephants on the astral realm, and on the causal realm you might have had a great feeling of belonging and loving. On the mental realm you might have been learning the principles of aerodynamics, and on the etheric you might have been in a pattern of self-realization. You come back to the waking state in the physical, bringing back a conglomerate memory of all these realms and experiences. It's no wonder some of your dreams appear to be confusing. The memory can be multidimensional and difficult to interpret. The best you can do is keep a record of all your dreams. As you have more experience with this, you will be able to separate the levels of consciousness and decipher your night travel experiences.

In reality, no one can interpret your dreams as well as you can. If someone else explains your dream to you, you ultimately have to accept or reject that interpretation. And if you are ultimately going to do it anyway, why not begin by learning to interpret your dreams for yourself?

You might go through your journal and highlight the symbols that recur in your dreams. A simple way of getting more information about a symbol is to "talk" to it as if it could speak to you directly. For some people, writing the conversation down works best; others find that they can hold imaginary conversations with the symbol and find out what the symbol represents for them and any information it carries. I know a young woman who had a dream of walking along a path that was blocked by a very large, black spider in a web. She woke up feeling a little frightened and concerned, but when she had calmed herself down, she held an imaginary conversation with both the path she was walking and the spider that was blocking it and came up with helpful information that she could work with in her daily life. The road she was walking on represented to her the spiritual path she had chosen, and she found that the spider was a part of herself that felt judged as being ugly and not good enough for that path. Her judgment and rejection of this part of herself was blocking her from making the progress she wanted to make. She took it a little further and, in asking what the spider wanted from her in order to let her pass, found that all she had to do was love that part of her that she considered ugly and unworthy. This fits with the spiritual teachings she had been studying, and has assisted her in being more accepting of herself. You may or may not want to go into that kind of detail with your dreams. This is just one of many tools you can use in getting conscious value from the night travel.

As you work with your dreams, your ability to understand what is of value to you can become a very rapid process. The investment of time as you start working with your dreams can lead to greater skill in your understanding. It is the same as learning in most areas; there is a learning curve, and the beginning stages take more time as you master the skills involved.

You have to be very careful that you separate the various realms and that you differentiate between illusion and reality. For example, there was a woman a while back who saw in a dream an earthquake that was devastating. She then predicted an earthquake, and her prediction was much publicized. The physical earthquake that she predicted never came about, but she died of a massive heart attack very close to the time she had predicted for the earthquake. She had projected her own death pattern and seen it as an earthquake. Many times, you project yourself into your dream patterns and then perceive that as an action separate from yourself. It's good to be aware of this and to separate your own projections from the reality of other dreams.

Earthquake dreams can also be symbolic of upheavals in emotions, and may herald significant changes in your environment. If you dream of earthquakes, you may not necessarily want to leave town to escape them. You might just want to watch for changes to occur in your life and realize that you have the opportunity to flow with those changes and to love yourself throughout the changes.

You might occasionally experience a dream within a dream where you "wake up" from one dream and find that you are still dreaming. The dream that you wake up from is usually pretty traumatic. The subconscious mind, working as a guardian, will break the pattern, and you will find yourself on another level. The subconscious mind will work to protect the consciousness from trauma. So when you have periods of time when you are not remembering your dreams, you might be wise not to force yourself into remembering. There may be a good reason for the memory to be temporarily blocked. Whenever you are working in this area, or any other area, remember to ask for the highest good.

There is a whole area of dreaming that has to do with communication with someone who has passed on: "I dreamed that my mother came into my room and told me to wake up because I had forgotten to lock the door. I got up and checked, and I had forgotten to lock the door." This happens when the person dreamed about is on the astral realm, which is so close to the physical realm that this type of direct communication can take place. It can also take place between two people who are both still living on the physical, and when it does, it usually means that one or the other is traveling in the astral body. This can happen whether or not the people are aware of it consciously.

People in MSIA who have loved ones on the spirit side have been taken many times in the dream state to the realm and level where the loved ones reside. There they have seen and communicated with the loved ones, and have realized that they were very much alive, not in the physical sense, but in the larger sense, well, healthy, happy, and contented with their present state of consciousness. The feeling of sadness that comes from being separated from the loved ones is often replaced with relief and joy, whether or not the dreamer is consciously aware of the visit in the dream state. Some people who do remember have asked me for verification. My question is, "Did it seem real at the time?" They'll usually say, "Oh, yes, very much so." If they think about it, they'll usually realize that, at that time, the physically awake state seemed pretty unreal. When you come back to the physical consciousness, the other realms seem unreal. But when you move out of this physical consciousness, the higher realms become more real than this one.

7

The Spiritual Value
of Dreaming

When you die in the physical world, you go to the spirit side as a progression in your evolvement. You go very nearly to the level of consciousness, the realm of Light, that you were able to manifest while you were here, and you might go just a little bit higher.

If you had progressed here as far as the causal level of consciousness, you would go to the causal realm. If you had progressed as far as the mental level of consciousness, you would go to the mental realm, and so on. If your consciousness is based in any of the lower realms, you are still bound by the law of cause and effect, and you must move again into a physical, material existence to work out and fulfill those patterns, releasing yourself into the higher realms.

If you have established yourself in consciousness on the Soul level, you move into that realm, and the pattern of return is broken. Once you move above the fifth realm, into positive Spirit, you do not have to return again to the physical earth. Your own Soul stands as the judge and places you on the correct realm, on the appropriate level. There is no outside judge; your own Soul judges you—and so honestly that you can't cheat even a little bit. It knows everything you've done and thought and felt, so it can be completely fair. And it is completely fair.

I have given you a schematic norm for what happens during the night travel. The possibilities and variations are infinite. Just as there are more than five billion people on the planet, there are more than five billion ways to experience the dream state. Your experiences won't be quite the same as anyone else's. They will be your own, individual to you.

Some people, for example, may bypass the stage of twilight sleep. The other levels of consciousness may move away from the physical in any order and do not necessarily move in the order I've indicated. You may have all of these processes taking place in one night, or only one or two. Because your various levels of consciousness travel in one particular pattern on Monday night does not necessarily mean that they will repeat that pattern on Tuesday night. The process may vary tremendously from time to time. You may experience night travel for only part of your sleeping time, and the consciousness may be comparatively dormant during the rest of your sleep. The dreams and travel may take a short amount of time, or all night. Your meaningful experiences may come shortly after you go to sleep, in the early hours of the morning, or just before you get up. Do you get the idea? There is no one way. There are many ways. You have to discover your own.

Some people dream around three or four o'clock in the morning, and when it's time to get up, they can't remember their dreams. It becomes difficult to keep a record of them. If you dream around four o'clock, set your alarm clock for that time. Wake up and write down your dreams; then give yourself the suggestion that "tomorrow morning, I'd like to have dreams at five o'clock." The next day, set the clock for five o'clock. When it wakes you up, write down your dreams and suggest to yourself that you'd like to have the dreams around six o'clock the next morning. You can move yourself and your dream pattern ahead this way. Within a couple of weeks, you should be able to dream in the early morning hours, just before you get up, so when you wake up, you can write down your dreams and have a pretty clear memory of them.

If writing down the dreams causes difficulty, you can experiment with other ways of recording your dreams. You might try putting a tape recorder by your bed and talking the dreams into the tape recorder, if that works better for you. There are no restrictions on using the things that will work for you. Whatever way will increase your spiritual awareness, use it.

When you learn the techniques of expanding your consciousness (and recording your dreams is an important one), you can be aware of all levels of consciousness at the same time, with an awareness that is as real as the awareness you have of the physical right now. This multidimensional awareness comes with a realization and a knowing and a being; it does not come from thinking or mentalizing about this material.

The dream state, the night travel on the spirit side, is a learning experience. It is a progression of your consciousness into the higher levels of Light. Your freedom lies in the Soul consciousness. When you reach Soul, you can go even higher into the center of the supreme God and become a co-worker with God. The progression that is open to you is endless and infinite. As you travel above the Soul realm, you come into total awareness—or God consciousness—and you experience the great Ocean of Love and Mercy. There are no words for these experiences. You have to experience them to have the understanding of them. You have to do this for yourself. I can't do it for you, let alone tell you.

You must find the truth within yourself. You move into and through all the levels of consciousness. No matter what, you don't stop; you continue the progression. If you keep moving, you cannot be bound by illusion. As soon as you stop and say, "This is it," the illusions will be there to put you in bondage. Keep going—always.

The night travel is the training ground for handling illusions. Through the dream process, you can learn to recognize and bypass the illusions continually. These are your lessons of unfoldment. Use them. You work these things by yourself. Your spiritual development is individual. I can point out the way. I can be a wayshower. I can travel with you and stand by you. I can clarify things for you and support you and guide you, if you let me.

The Traveler is with you always, but cannot do it for you. You must bring to yourself conscious guidance and direction if you are to move forward on the path of your spiritual inner awareness and the path of your spiritual evolvement through the lower worlds into the realms of pure Spirit, where you reside in the freedom of your own Soul consciousness.

8

The Flame Meditation

The flame meditation is designed to release many of the emotional areas of your consciousness. It's a good meditation to do if you have been feeling irritated, upset, angry, or otherwise out of balance emotionally.

The flame meditation deals with the very specific, powerful energies of fire. Fire is always a two-edged sword. It can be used for great good, as when it is used to provide warmth, cook food, for construction, and to decorate and beautify. Out of control, however, fire is one of the most destructive forces that exists. I approach any meditation that uses fire as its focal point with extreme caution. I suggest that you always respect the force with which you are working and use common sense in your handling of the fire.

Practicing the flame meditation can directly affect your dream state. It will usually heighten your awareness of your dreams. You may bring back much greater memory of your dreams after doing this meditation, and they may be of an unusual nature. You may dream of fire, and you may feel emotional turmoil within your dreaming. Don't let it disturb you. The emotions are releasing; you are receiving emotional balancing. That's one of the greatest values of this technique.

Because this is such a powerful technique, I suggest that you approach it cautiously. The first time, do it for no more than five or ten minutes. The energies this exercise brings in and the emotional patterns it releases are much more dynamic than you may be used to handling. Do the meditation for five or ten minutes, then watch your dream pattern and your emotional balance closely. If things are a little unusual or a little shaky, don't do the meditation again for several days. Give things a chance to settle down and come back into balance. Then do it again. If everything seems to be flowing along okay, go ahead and do the meditation for a little longer. Continue to watch the dream patterns and the emotions. If things are shaky, let it go for a few days and then do it again when you feel back in balance. As you become accustomed to these higher energies, you'll be able to hold the meditation for longer periods of time. I suggest that you never do the flame meditation for longer than twenty minutes a day. That is a lot, and you will get all that you might need from that period of time. Any more than that may not be beneficial for you.

To do the meditation, find a candle that is taller than the holder the candle is in so that you can clearly see the flame. It doesn't matter what type of candle you use. You can use tapered candles, thick candles, or little votive candles. They're all fine, as long as the candle is not set so deeply into a holder that you have to look down on the flame. You want to clearly see the flame while you are looking forward.

During the meditation, you want the candle flame to be at about eye level. You can either hold the candle or set it down on something, as long as it is at eye level. If you can, it's better to find a place to set it down. It eliminates the risk of dropping the candle as you move into the meditation. Never do the flame meditation in bed or in a place where there is a fire danger. Always blow the candle out as soon as you have finished the part of the meditation that uses the flame.

Once you have the candle and the place for your meditation ready, light the candle, sit down and get comfortable, and invoke a prayer of Light for your own protection. Ask that the meditation bring forward only those things that are for your highest good. It isn't necessary, but you may want to have soft music playing in the background. It may help you hold a point of focus, a reference point for the mind and its rhythm.

Begin gazing at the candle flame, placing your consciousness forward into that point of light. Just observe what takes place in and around the flame, and observe the sensations and reactions in your body. It is very important that, while you are gazing at the flame, you do not allow yourself to slip into a trance-like state. It's easy to do with this exercise. It is very necessary that you keep the energy flowing forward and out toward the flame, or flowing up. Don't allow the energy to drop down within your consciousness. If you feel the energy starting to drop back or fade back inward, blow out the candle and stop the meditation immediately. These energies are not to be misused.

The trance state is not the most positive or uplifting state of being. It will not bring about the positive release of emotional imbalance. It could, indeed, compound the imbalance and confuse the consciousness. So it is extremely important that you monitor this potential carefully. Keep the energy flowing up and out, and stop the meditation immediately if you feel the energy dropping inward.

You will know. You'll be able to feel it if you are slipping into a trance. If you can pull the energy back up and focus it outwardly into the flame, that's fine. If you can't, stop the meditation.

While gazing at the flame, emotional areas may begin stirring within you. You may enter into powerful feelings of disturbance and despair as the turmoil of your life is brought up to be purified in the fire of Spirit, which the flame symbolizes. Just observe the feelings as they appear, hold your concentration on the flame, and release all those feelings into the Light. Become a neutral channel through which the emotions may flow out and be cleansed.

You may feel a pulling or pulsating sensation in the area of the eyes, between the eyes, and in the head. The eyes may tear. The vision may blur. It's all part of the process of releasing and lifting into areas of higher perception and awareness.

As you gaze at the flame, you may notice that it shoots up very high or flickers almost violently for a time, and then burns back down again. That may happen only occasionally or as a repeated pattern. There are a few possible causes. One is that there is something within the candle wick that is causing the flame to flicker and burn irregularly. You may want to change candles if it distracts you. If it's not the wick, it may be that you're blowing on the candle as you breathe out, causing it to flicker. You can hold the candle far enough away from you that you don't blow on it, or you can breathe gently so that there is no disturbance. If it's neither the wick nor your breath, it may be the energy present that is causing the candle to flicker and burn with an unusually tall flame. It may just be the power of your consciousness as it is projected into the flame. As you focus and send energy into the flame, you may be able to make it shoot up several inches and then bring it right back down again as you redirect the energy. It will give you an indicator for what you are doing.

The candle flame will burn off extra amounts of energy. This is one reason why it's often nice to have a candle burning in your home. It will burn and transmute excess energy. It's particularly helpful if family members or friends who are visiting are expressing emotional turmoil. When this is happening, they are releasing excess energy into the environment. Having a candle burning can help to balance them and keep you clear of picking up their negative energy.

The flame has an energy field. As you gaze at it, you may begin to perceive the colors of this energy field. You may see the colors on the outside of the flame, following the shape of the flame closely. Or you may see a circular glow encompassing, but also extending beyond, the flame itself. You may see a circular glow at the tip of the flame or in the heat pattern above the flame. The primary colors you'll see will be green, blue, and red. As you tune into the spiritual frequency, you may see purple. You might even see a rainbow of colors within the flame.

There is a devic force that works with the flame. It is a life force, a consciousness that is from the devic kingdom (which is a lower part of the angelic kingdom), and it is part of the fire's existence. Remember the Bible story of the prophet who was thrown into the furnace to burn? An angel appeared and protected him so that he was not harmed, even in the midst of the fire. This was a form of fire elemental or fire angel. They exist, and they have dominion over fire. They can control it and all its functions. There are people who are attuned to these fire forms and who can work with them. I've known people who could take burns away from the body because they worked with the fire lords. In ancient cultures, people almost always worshipped fire gods. In Hawaii, the god of the volcano was worshipped, which is a form of fire god. These forces definitely do exist, and communication with them can be established.

As you gaze at the candle flame, you may see the fire deva appear. It usually looks like a little figure, almost human in shape, but it is made of fire. It may appear to have arms, legs, and a head, although it may flicker and twist as the flame does. It may appear to be transparent. You may see it along the edge of the flame or at the tip, even sometimes slightly above the tip of the flame or in the darker area of the center. It may appear and hold steady for a moment or may just flash in momentarily. Some people have described it as a little man with a head and arms, but no legs. Some have described it as just an unusual light within the flame that flickers from one side to the other. Some have seen it in such detail that they've even seen the features of its face. Everybody's experience with this seems to be different. You may see it or you may not. If you do, you'll have a reference point for what it is.

It is interesting to note that the only restriction people have is their doubt and lack of confidence in their ability to do all things. There are no restrictions on your consciousness, which is why you can move into this meditation and have success. The consciousness of the fire deva is restricted. It must stay within the energy pattern from which it takes its existence. But you can move your consciousness there and tap into its beingness. You can communicate with it on its terms. You can move into any energy pattern and perceive it directly. You are flexible. You are multidimensional. But you must develop your awareness of the totality of your beingness. This and other meditations that I have shared[3] are valuable because they expand your awareness of all the levels of your existence and increase your flexibility in traveling from one state of consciousness to another.

As you watch the flame, you may find yourself moving into an almost dreamlike state, even while you are meditating. It's okay to follow along with the images that come forward, as long as you keep the energy flowing up and out. Observe the images, and direct them outward toward the flame. You may be reminiscing about your daily life, about things that happened when you were a little younger, and then back to things that happened when you were a child. You may keep going back to earlier and earlier times in your life, and suddenly move out of this existence and into another one. You may find that you are remembering things that did not happen to you in this existence. You may be tapping into the records of your previous existences, which can happen through this meditation. Allow yourself to flow

3. Other meditations by John-Roger are available in his book, INNER WORLDS OF MEDITATION. Many meditations by John-Roger are also available on audiotape. See "Suggested Study Materials for Further Study" at the end of the book for more information.

along with this experience and, as the images appear, just let them go. Release them into the flame and see them purified and cleansed from your consciousness.

If your eyelids start feeling heavy and closing, or when your time for observing the candle flame is over, blow out your candle, sit back, and drop into a quiet meditation. With your eyes closed, observe whatever appears on the screen of your inner eye. Keep your legs and arms uncrossed so that the power can flow freely. You may see a lot of shapes or forms or strange lights. Let it all float through. You don't even have to wonder what it is. You may see the flame deva during this part of the meditation, too. Just acknowledge its presence and send it Light and love. If you see images from your past during this part of the meditation, bless them and yourself with the Light and let them go. Releasing these patterns can bring about great healing and balance.

After a few minutes of sitting quietly with your eyes closed, you will intuitively sense when the energy of the meditation lifts and the meditation is over. If you feel unfocused or find it difficult to move around, you might say the tone "E" inwardly or out loud a couple of times. Say it as a sustained "EEEEEEE" sound, starting the voice at a very low pitch and visualizing it down around your feet, then taking it up to a very high pitch, visualizing it moving up through the body to the top of the head, and then back down to a low pitch at the feet again. Chanting this tone a couple of times can realign all your energies and anchor you back on this physical level.

Once you have read all of the information about the flame meditation, you may want to use the following step-by-step overview to assist you in doing the meditation.

1. Find a candle that is taller than its holder.
2. Set the candle where you can see the flame at eye level, or hold the candle at eye level.
3. Call in the Light for your protection and highest good to come forward.
4. Begin gazing at the candle flame at about eye level, keeping your energy flowing out toward the flame.
5. Observe the flame and your body, mind, and emotions, allowing whatever happens to release into the Light.
6. If you find your energy dropping down or inward, either refocus your energy outward toward the flame, or blow out the candle and stop the meditation.
7. Do the meditation for five or ten minutes at first, building up to a maximum of twenty minutes.

8. Blow out the candle, close your eyes and sit quietly for a few minutes to complete the meditation.
9. To center yourself back in the body, chant the "E" inwardly or out loud a couple of times. Say it as a sustained "EEEEEEE" sound, starting the voice at a very low pitch and visualizing it down around your feet, then taking it up to a very high pitch, visualizing it moving up through the body to the top of the head, and then back down to a low pitch at the feet again.
10. Observe your emotions. If you feel emotionally shaky, wait a day or two until you feel balanced before doing the meditation again.
11. Be aware of your dreams. The clearing started in this meditation can continue in the dream state, and the energy of the meditation may cause greater remembrance of your dreams. If there is disturbance in the dreams, wait until they have settled down and then do the meditation again.

9

Questions & Answers

Q: I am confused about dreams and Soul travel. Are they the same thing?

A: There are lower levels of consciousness: physical, astral, causal, mental and etheric. These are all below the level of Soul. This might be what is called "worlds without end." You can travel in these levels and remain within your own consciousness, never traveling outside of your own inner domain. What is generally called dreaming takes place in these levels.

On the Soul level and above, there is no dreaming defined as such. In those levels, you are involved in awareness.

Q: How do I move into those levels of awareness more?

A: You tell yourself before you go to sleep that you'd like to move into those awarenesses more. That's the answer.

Q: Are there any signposts, other than the sounds and the colors of the realms, that would give me feedback that I am in those levels above the Soul?

A: There are sounds that can be heard above the level of Soul. Colors blend and become clear, so that becomes difficult to perceive. You might meet some beings who would give you information that you've never had before. Things may be said to you, or you may see things which you don't know how to understand or perceive. They won't be like anything that you know at this point, so you'll have no reference point for them. When you return to the awake state here in the physical, you write that down. If it shows up again, you write it down again. It's a process of becoming familiar with it, which means being exposed to it many, many times. There may not be anything you can do with it *here,* because it's not *here.*

As you go into the other levels, you may start recognizing certain places or building-type structures because you have seen them a lot. It's a process of repetition, doing a certain procedure that takes you to this signpost again and again. It may be a symbol that you pass many times, and you begin to realize that you've seen that symbol a lot. There are ways, just too many for me to even try to give you one or two. I end up giving you so many that you get swamped with the ways. I do know that the best way is to just keep at it.

If you're trying to understand the Spirit from this level, there's just no way you're going to do it. How would you fit a 747 jumbo jet into this room? You just wouldn't. It doesn't fit. It doesn't work to do that here. You have to go to the airport to see it. While you're here, you can think about it. The only way you can get it into this room is as a symbol through your thoughts and imagination. But you're not going to get *it* into this room. You only get *it* there. You have to go where it is.

Q: I understand that there are a couple of things happening at night: one is dreaming, which may or may not have anything to do with Soul transcendence, and one is night travel. The value in recording and working with dreams is that we can learn about things that may happen in the future and we can see how we're clearing things that happen during daily life. The value of watching what's happening in the states of awareness is becoming aware of our spiritual progression. Am I on track?
A: So far.

Q: You also said to watch for the colors in the Spirit realms to know where we are. I haven't had the experience of being aware enough in my dreams to say, "Oh, now it's time to ask for the Traveler," or "This is where I watch for the colors." How can I develop that ability?

A: You set the program before you start doing s.e.'s, or before you go to sleep. Before I drive somewhere, I put the Light around me to surround and protect me, and I send it down the road ahead of me. Then I drive it. Along the way I make all sorts of choices about what roads I drive on, but I'm still on my way to Los Angeles or wherever I'm going. If traffic gets heavy, I may stop for dinner and start driving again a little later when traffic is lighter. This is the same thing that you're talking about. There are all sorts of things that you do after making your initial selection. Just as situations out in the world are constantly changing, things inside of you are changing all the time, also. You're constantly re-evaluating and re-adapting. You've got to be flexible and work with what is present.

Q: What does tracking my dreams have to do with my spiritual exercises, or more to the point, my spiritual awareness and progression?

A: There are many forms of spiritual exercises. It's a state of forcing yourself to be aware. If you go to sleep by midnight, and then wake yourself at 2:30 in the morning, there is a chance that you will be closer in contact with that other level that knows the dreams, and you could be pulling those across because there is less confusion in the mind.

If you want to find out where you are in your levels of spirituality, keep track of what you dream about. That will tell you where you are. Generally speaking, if you are dreaming about sex, food, your job, your spouse, or any number of material concerns, you will be incarnating back to those levels. Regardless of the level of initiation you have reached, you are going to pull yourself back to this level. Some of you dream with the Traveler, moving into other levels of consciousness and working things out. You are bringing balance to past actions. You are involved in it and you know it. Your awareness of this process lets you see your level of progression.

Q: A lot of my dreams are from my everyday life. It feels like I just can't quite get away from all the concerns of the day. Do you have any suggestions for how to clear my mind better so my focus could be more on spiritual things?
A: There is a technique called free-form writing which can help clear the subconscious and unconscious levels. I explain this process in detail in the "Living In Grace"[4] packet, which I suggest you listen to, and I'll give you a brief explanation here.

4. LIVING IN GRACE. See the listing of suggested materials for further study at the back of the book.

Set yourself up with a pen and a good supply of paper where you will not be disturbed while you are doing this exercise. You might unplug the phone, close your door, and tell the people you live with not to disturb you for a while. Light a candle, call in the Light, and start writing down the thoughts that come into your mind. You are not just letting the pen do the writing, as in automatic writing. This is a process of you writing down whatever is in your mind. You might not be able to finish writing each thought or word. It doesn't matter if what you write make sense or not; just keep writing down whatever comes into your mind. If you can't think of anything to write, write that down: "I can't think of anything to write."

This will start to release patterns of the unconscious. As they come up, they can carry tremendous levels of emotion, and you may find yourself writing very forcefully. That's why I recommend that you use a pen rather than a pencil, where you might break the lead and have to stop your train of thought to go sharpen it. You can't do this exercise in shorthand, nor on a computer or typewriter, because that's not how you put the information into your consciousness to begin with.

You may release things symbolically and find that pressures and obsessive behaviors let go. Don't even question what they are; just let it all go. You don't want to find and reactivate things that are clearing from your consciousness. I suggest that you not think back over what you have written or talk about it to anyone else. If you do, you might put things back into your consciousness again, and it can be very difficult to clear them out the second time.

When you get through, do *not* go back and reread any of what you have written. Rip it up and, if you can, burn it. This will complete the releasing process. After a while, just fifteen minutes may be enough to clear your consciousness, though you may start out writing for one or two or more hours. Write until you feel a peace come in.

Free-form writing is a good way to wedge deeply into these areas. It's like cutting into an onion, slicing wedges into the center. The Light will start getting in there and, like the onion, the wedges will dry up and fall away. You'll often feel a sense of freedom as you move away from the materiality of the physical world.

Q: I've heard you say that we Soul travel all the time. Does that mean that when I go blank and kind of space out, my Soul is out traveling somewhere?
A: It can. It can also just be a sign that you've run out of information.

Q: Are there any other signs to know if I am Soul traveling?

A: You listen for the Sound Current and you look inside to see what colors appear. That will usually tell you what level the Soul is moving out on.

Q: If I'm not yet seeing or hearing inside, then can I assume that I am traveling?

A: Yes. When I'm not aware that I'm breathing, I still assume that I'm breathing. I find that I breathe all the time, even when I'm not focused on it, so I assume that I'm breathing whether or not I'm paying attention to that. It's an accurate assumption. What you're dealing with is becoming more aware that that is taking place. You can transfer that information directly to Soul traveling.

Q: I understand that we go to school during the dream state. What are we learning? Do we have a choice in the curriculum, or how is all that decided?

A: Only those who work within a spiritual discipline that works during the dream state go to school during that time. Those people learn what they are capable of receiving. Each person goes at their own rate of progress. Spirit will not inflict on you, so you are never given more than you can handle. In essence, you make your choice of the curriculum by your choice of how you express loving and how you avoid the loving expression, past and present.

Q: I don't seem to remember my dreams. Will this block my spiritual progress?
A: Probably not. If a dream is really important, you'll generally remember it. There are a lot of dreams that aren't important to remember, although they might assist you if you do learn to bring the memory back. There are several techniques that are helpful in remembering. Probably the most effective thing to do is to write down the dreams that you do remember. Keep a journal. As you attune yourself to your dreaming, you'll start to remember more.

Q: If I am not remembering what's happened during the sleep state, is just as much taking place?
A: Yes. Look at it this way: you're not aware of what's happening on 42nd Street and Broadway in New York, but there is still a lot going on there.

Q: So my level of awareness doesn't really change my Soul transcendence ability?
A: I worked with a woman who never had any conscious experience of any of the spiritual levels. She just said, "I believe you; I trust you." She got initiated through all the levels, never had a conscious

experience, never saw the Light, never did anything. She read her discourses, listened to tapes, kept a diary, kept a this and kept a that, and she liked it. She got initiated to the Soul level and it all clicked into place. She never had another conscious experience for a long time after that, but she just keeps on going because that's what we're going to do anyway. She had the experiences all right; it's just that she had no awareness of them.

Q: When I pay attention to my dreams and record them, I remember so much that it can take me an hour or more every morning to write it all down, and I don't know what to do with all of it. It gets to the point where I'd be spending a lot of my waking time remembering and trying to understand what happened while I was asleep, and that seems silly. Do you have any suggestions on how to work with this?

A: The good news is that you have the flow going from the sleep state into this waking state on the physical. You can now start asking, before you go to sleep at night, that you bring back information and experiences in a clear way that you can understand easily. Then, instead of bringing back a long story, your consciousness may start bringing you just the "punch line." You may start waking up with the awareness that you were involved in clearing past actions, or being of assistance somewhere, or learning something new that may or may not relate to this level. You may just wake up knowing that you need to handle certain things that day, or that it's a day for you to focus on a certain part of your expression, etc. You can start moving into the phase of bringing back awarenesses. It is still helpful to write things down; that will help you to track your progress and growth in this area.

Q: I understand that you encourage people to keep a dream journal and to read back over it at times to help understand how the dreams relate to our daily life. I am pretty sure that some of my dreams are clearing things, and I am afraid that I will just put those things back into my consciousness if I reread my dreams. It all seems like old stuff that I either don't understand or don't want to remember anyway. Can you explain this a little more to me?

A: It is true that many things can be cleared in the dream state when you are working with the Traveler. And rereading those things can recycle them into your consciousness. An important factor here is intention. If you are rereading your dreams for understanding, there is less chance that you will pick something up. However, since you have this concern, it may be wise for you to tear up the dreams that seem like clearings to you, and not reread them. It is not necessary that you keep all the dreams. If something is important for you to know and understand, it will show up again in another dream.

Before you go to sleep, you might ask that any information that is beneficial for you to know be given in a form that you can easily understand. You may also ask that you only remember those dreams that are beneficial for you to remember. You don't necessarily need to remember everything. Many times the Traveler, or your own consciousness, does not allow you memory of things that have been cleared because that would not be for your upliftment.

Q: When I'm doing s.e.'s, my mind just doesn't stop. It goes on and on about all kinds of things, even how I have to pay attention to my s.e.'s. Will that affect my awareness in the night travel?

A: One thing you can do in your s.e.'s is get a little tape recorder and click it on when your mind comes up with something, record it, and then put the recorder on hold. Your mind can then let go of the situation. You need to go back and listen to the tape, and either go do the things or find out why you don't have to do them. Otherwise, these things will probably start showing up in the night travel as your consciousness tries to get them worked out.

Q: How do I work with my unawareness to bring in more awareness?

A: You have to find out when and under what circumstances you go into unawareness. If you go unaware doing s.e.'s lying down, sit up. If you do it sitting, do your s.e.'s standing up. Then if you go unaware, you'll experience falling and that will wake you up in a hurry. It will bring in the awareness. Each time, you'll invade the unawareness more and more with your conscious awareness. You'll be keeping yourself more aware as you move into those areas of sleep.

This is also part of the value of recording your dreams. The act of bridging the inner levels from the night travel into this physical level strengthens and expands your awareness into areas that were previously unavailable to you consciously. The bridging of the inner and outer consciousness is of great value when you start to bring back awarenesses from your travels in the "high country."

Q: Is it possible that the unawareness I sometimes experience is a form of protection? Could it be better for me to not bring back remembrance of the dreams sometimes? How can I know the difference between that and just being lazy?

A: The fact that you're asking these questions doesn't sound like laziness. It sounds like you're ready to confront the thing head on.

Q: I would really like to. I'm wondering if I'm doing, or not doing, something that's causing the unawareness.

A: Self-inquiry is the foremost way to become aware. You ask yourself, "Why am I unaware? Why am I not participating in this?" You may get an immediate answer, or you may get no answer at all because you're not ready to be taught what that is. When you're ready to be taught, you become the student to the information instead of trying to get the information and then become the master of it. Information can't come to a master because they've already claimed that they know. Someone who's ordinary, however, will acknowledge ignorance. Not knowing is being open to receive the information. Once you receive it, there's a good chance that you can do something with it. If you don't receive the information, you can't do anything with it, and you won't know which way to turn to make something happen. Letting go, asking inside, and a willingness to just be open will help a great deal.

Q: When I am traveling through the inner realms of Light in the dream state, will the dreams appear as a color form?
A: They could, but most of the time we bring dreams back into the physical memory in story form. The lower self screens the dream experiences and brings them back to you in ways that you can readily relate

to. You might remember Soul traveling as driving in a car up a hill. That's travel as you understand it on this physical level. Of you might remember getting on a plane and flying somewhere, but you don't remember where. You might remember being with a group of people at a seminar. It may not have happened that way in the spiritual state, but you have to have some way to relate it to your physical experience. The storyteller inside of you will translate the spiritual experiences into physical-level symbols.

Q: *What does it mean when I see you, the physical form of John-Roger, in my dreams?*
A: When you see me in a dream, it could mean a lot of things. It could be a mock-up from your subconscious telling you what you want to know. It could be symbolic of your high self or your spiritual self. It could be the Traveler being there in a very specific and direct experience. And it could mean that the Traveler is supporting you in whatever is going on at that moment.

It really doesn't matter which it is, because you're going to go on, regardless. If it's your own mock-up, so what? You're going to go beyond that. If you get information that doesn't check out in your waking life, then don't use that information. Just say, "That doesn't work for me." Where that information came from really isn't an issue at that point.

On the other hand, if the information *does* work for you, then use it. It doesn't matter if it came from the Traveler or from your own subconscious.

If the experience is a direct experience of being present with the Traveler, that's terrific. And you're going to have to continue on once the experience is over, so there's no use getting attached to it. If it means that spiritual support is with you, that's nice, too. You're going to have to move on to the next experience. The dreams can be a lot of things, and you must always check out the validity of anything through your own experience in your daily life.

Q: I sometimes see members of the MSIA staff in my dreams, but I never see you. Is something wrong?
A: The Traveler will often use forms that you are familiar with and with whom you feel a rapport to communicate with you. When you get more familiar with the Traveler's spiritual form and feel more comfortable with that, then the other forms will disappear and you will see the form of the Traveler directly. There is nothing wrong with your current experience.

Q: You recently came to me in a dream. You were standing on my right and gave me some information. How do I validate that what you told me was accurate?

A: If you receive information that seems totally out of character for you or if I tell you something that is not what you have experienced of my teachings, write to me about the experience. Information that is out of character might be "leave your husband" or "stand in front of a moving car." If it's information that you can use to lift yourself, check it out. I always tell you to lean into information that you receive. That's how you can validate for yourself the information in the tapes and publications as well as information that you might get in dreams.

Q: *When I dream about you, there's always a lot of humor involved, lots of laughing before and during seminars, and really funny situations. I'm curious about that.*
A: One of the signs of the presence of the Spirit, or I say the Traveler, is great joy and humor. When I was a kid, my friends and I would often be hit with great peals of laughter in church at seemingly inappropriate times. The more inappropriate it was, the harder it was not to laugh until we'd all be guffawing and we'd have to get up and walk out to save respect for our families. Now some people get what they call a "tickle". Once that tickle goes off, it just doesn't matter where they are, here it comes. That's just how this thing works. A lot of us who have experienced this have also been told that we'll be punished in

some way if we do it again. You can feel this thing coming on, and the more you try to control or stifle it, the more it bursts through. *It* is in control. I know I never was when it happened to me. It taught me at a very early stage to cooperate with it. It's moving and it's joyful. Sometimes it's real raucous and in another way it can be real serene, but it's still very funny. It gets to the point where anything that anyone says or does just sets it off.

Q: Sometimes when this laughter hits, I feel embarrassed, or I really start to sweat. Is it possible that past actions are being balanced and released, or that I am breaking free of patterns through this?

A: "Free" is another term, but yes, you certainly can release yourself from past actions through laughter. Even in your daily life, if you can laugh instead of taking umbrage at some of the things that people say or do, then you are already free at that moment and the situation can't hang on you. HUMOR starts with HU, which is more like God, or God more. So the more laughter and joy there are, the more you're in the presence of the Spirit.

Q: When I have dreams with other people that involve my own desires and wishes about them, how can I know if the people are actually there, or if this is just wish fulfillment on my part?

A: The other person will probably not be there because you have mocked up their consciousness from within your own inner levels of desire. If you are having an actual out-of- body experience, which is an awareness state on another level, then they may be there in reality. However, it is rare that your own body desires would promote themselves against you on those other levels.

Q: *I've been having a lot of bad dreams at night. When I wake up, I'm really frightened, and it can take hours to get myself back into balance and to sleep again. Can you suggest anything?*

A: Your dreams could be all sorts of things: balancing past actions, working through unconscious or subconscious fears or blocks, etc., particularly when the Traveler Consciousness is working with you. Whatever they are, don't give them a lot of power. If you wake up after a bad dream, just go to work with yourself. Chant your tone or the HU or the Ani-Hu. Surround yourself with the Light. Ask for the Traveler to help you release the dream experience. Keep some water by your bed and drink a little of it to help break the intensity of the dream experience and to help you come back into the body.

There is also a tone of "E" that you can chant which will help to bring you back into the physical focus. You just say, "EEEEEEEE"—a long, drawn out sound. You start the sound low, and imagine it down around your feet. Then you take it up as high as you can, and imagine it up at the top of the head. Then drop it back down as low as you can, back down to the feet. That will help to bring you back solidly into the physical level in a balanced way.

Exercise can also break the unbalanced feeling from "bad dreams," so you might do whatever sort of exercise works for you. Doing a few sit-ups, dancing to a little music, or walking around are a few possibilities. Just do something to get the body energy moving and to help shift your focus.

Q: I often wake up with a cotton-head, a real heaviness in my head and eyes. Is this necessarily something that's happening during the night travel, and if so, is there some way I can protect myself during the night travel?
A: Most of the time, the things from the Spirit world don't get across here. I would check the physical level first. There are doctors and practitioners who can check and see if you have allergies or a high level of toxicity in your system. I've given some suggestions before on how to clear yourself after having a nightmare: exercise, drink a little water, etc. These may assist with what you're talking about, too.

I would also look to see if you are going to sleep in a state of denial. If so, you'll wake up in a state of denial. It can transfer across into something else, and plug up the thinking and the head because denial will do that. It's a form of self-protection. Ask yourself, "What am I denying?" Maybe just start randomly saying things, and see if something clicks in for you. Then I would look at why you are denying that thing. Another way to look at it is to ask yourself, "What do I expect should take place?" What do I think this should look like rather than what it is? You may just realize that you're overly sensitive.

Ask yourself these questions, and move into acknowledging the information. It's a form of honesty. You're not dealing with good or bad, just information. Then you don't have to react against it. Start to move on what you can.

Q: In my dreams, I sometimes see people standing to my left. I've heard that if something comes in from the left, it is negative. The experiences I've had, however, have all been positive. Can you clarify this for me?

A: The negative power comes in from the left, but not everything that comes in from the left is negative. You've been told that . When something appears, all you do is chant your initiation tone, the HU or Ani-Hu.[5] If it's negative, it will disappear; it cannot stay in the presence of the positive energy of these tones. If it is not negative, then it will stay, and that's fine. It may even stand and chant your tone back to you, and that's also fine. You just know that it came in from the left.

A lot of things have come from the right that have raised holy hell with you and you wonder if that wasn't the negative power. No, it wasn't. Raising hell with you was to get you up to a new level that you were to go to. You were hanging on to the old, and it seemed like a struggle to get you to stand up straight. You fought the change, but now you're up and going, and you can use that as a reference point for the next changes that come your way. Let go and move with the changes as they come forward. You have sometimes looked at this as a form of punishment, but it is not. It's a form of discipline.

Q: What relationship, if any, do dreams have to past or future existences?
A: If you're working with a Master who works in the dream state, your dreams may be the resolving or balancing of past actions. They may also reflect some past impression or anxieties about the future. The

5. From *Inner Worlds of Meditation* by John-Roger. For further information, see the SUGGESTED MATERIALS FOR FURTHER STUDY section at the back of the book.

dreamer is the best interpreter of his or her own dreams. The most important thing is to live your physical, awake life in caring responsibility. If you are working with the Mystical Traveler Consciousness, ask the Traveler to work with you in the dream state before you go to sleep.

Q: Can you recommend any further reading material to assist me with understanding my dreams?
A: In general, dream interpretation is best done by the dreamer. No outside source can offer the validity and accuracy that you can about your own experience. You are the only one who can KNOW what your dreams mean to you. If you tune in to your dreams, write them down, review them later in the light of what has taken place in your life since the time of your dream, etc., then the interpretation will become clear for you. The more you do this, the more in tune with the process you become. You will be able to interpret your dreams more quickly and accurately with practice.

Q: Is there a way that I can become more attuned to the Christ consciousness through my dreams?
A: Ask. As you go to sleep at night, you can ask that you be more attuned to that consciousness of the Christ. You can also ask that the Traveler work with you in whatever way is for your highest good and

that you remember that which is beneficial for you to remember, in a way that you can understand. Then, when you wake up, you write down your dreams, or your sense of what went on in the dream state. Use all of this for your advancement. You can really set yourself up for success in having greater and greater awareness of the inner realms, and all of it can lead you to awareness of your Soul and the Soul realm if that is what you want and where you want to go.

Baruch Bashan.

(The blessings already are.)

SUGGESTED MATERIALS FOR FURTHER STUDY

LIVING IN GRACE
A Journey Home to the Heart of God
Six tapes of seminars, meditations and an innerphasing by John-Roger. Instructions for using an Innerphasing are included.
◆ *Free Form Writing*
◆ *Meditation on Forgiveness*
◆ *Are you Living Under Law or Grace?*
◆ *Forgiveness Innerphasing*
◆ *The Consciousness of Grace*
◆ *Meditation for Peace*
These tapes can be shared.
#3903, $49 cassette album

INNER WORLDS OF MEDITATION
J-R shares many meditation techniques in this book, as well as general information about the process of meditation and the inner realms of consciousness that can be reached by going within.
#977-7, $5 paperback

SOUL JOURNEY
THROUGH SPIRITUAL EXERCISES

Three tapes and a booklet, including:

◆ *Meditation for Soul Travel*
◆ *HU Chant & Breathing Exercise*
◆ *Human Spiritual Rights*

#3718, $30 cassette album

THE HU MEDITATION

J-R explains the HU chant and its significance and leads you in doing the meditation out loud and silently. An uplifting experience of Spirit's blessings.
#1800, $10 audio tape

MASTER CHOHANS OF THE COLOR RAYS

J-R discusses the different color frequencies and the masters who work with the color rays. This book can be a practical guide to using the color rays to enhance your life expression and awareness of the inner levels of consciousness.
#956-4, $8 paperback

CATHEDRAL OF THE SOUL

John-Roger presents some keys to active meditation and takes you on a beautiful meditative journey to the cathedral of your Soul.
#3714, $10 audio tape

INNER JOURNEY THROUGH SPIRIT REALMS
A guided meditation taking you through the physical, causal, mental, and etheric realms, and on through the cosmic mirror into the high country of your true self—the Soul.
#7251, $10 audio tape

All of the books and tapes listed above are available through MSIA. For more information or to order, please contact MSIA, P.O. Box 3935, Los Angeles, CA 90051, (213) 737-4055.

PEACE THEOLOGICAL SEMINARY & COLLEGE OF PHILOSOPHY®

Peace Theological Seminary and College of Philosophy (PTS) is a school through which the teachings that John-Roger offers are presented in class, workshop, and retreat formats. PTS offers a class on dreams in many areas throughout the world. This class is also offered in a home study format. For further information on the location nearest you, or to order the home study course, please contact PTS at 3500 W. Adams Blvd., Los Angeles, CA 90018, (213) 737-1534.

113

ABOUT JOHN-ROGER

For more than twenty-five years, John-Roger's life has been devoted to the spiritual work of Soul transcendence—the realization of oneself as a Soul and, more than that, as one with the Divine. In the course of this work, he has traveled and lectured extensively throughout the world, written over twenty books, and recorded hundreds of seminars, many of which are presented on his nationally seen television show, "That Which Is."

In addition, John-Roger has co-authored four books with Peter McWilliams: *You Can't Afford the Luxury of a Negative Thought, Life 101, Do It!—Let's Get Off Our Buts,* and *Wealth 101.* Both *Life 101* and *Do It!* have been New York Times bestsellers, with *Do It!* reaching #1 on the list. All four books present practical, down-to-earth suggestions for understanding and getting the most out of life.

John-Roger has also founded a number of organizations supporting such areas as education, health, and individual and world peace. The common thread throughout all of John-Roger's work is loving—of self, others, and God—and encouragement for each person to discover that loving within, for that is where God also dwells.

If you would like further information about the teachings offered by John-Roger through MSIA, please contact MSIA, P.O. Box 3935, Los Angeles, CA 90018, (213) 737-4055.

NOTES

NOTES

NOTES

NOTES

NOTES

NOTES

NOTES